MW01644516

THE IMPERIAL CHRONICLE

Volume One: Origins and Awakening

A Legacy of Power, Resilience, and Preservation

By Karena Apple Feng

First Edition

Published in the United States

ISBN: 9798290781297

Disclaimer: This work represents family oral tradition, personal spiritual experiences, and documented family history. While every effort has been made to ensure accuracy, some details reflect the author's understanding of family heritage and should be considered as memoir rather than formal historical documentation.

FORMAL DEDICATION

To the Dragon Spirits of Our Ancestors and Their Living Legacy

---

DEDICATION PREAMBLE

THIS DEDICATION is hereby established and set forth on this day as a **binding testament** of gratitude, recognition, and **active commission** for future action.

ARTICLE I: RECOGNITION OF ANCESTRAL SACRIFICE

BE IT KNOWN that the Dragon Spirits of our ancestral lineage **voluntarily relinquished** their visible legacy, thereby:

- **Transforming** recognition into resilience
- **Converting** immediate power into generational survival
- **Establishing** foundations for future emergence

- **Ensuring** the preservation of miracles through strategic concealment

THEREFORE, this dedication **acknowledges and honors** their supreme sacrifice as the **cornerstone** upon which all subsequent achievement rests.

ARTICLE II: SPECIFIC DEDICATION TO EDWARD KAO-MING FENG

BE IT RECORDED that **Edward Kao-Ming Feng**, born 1931, is hereby **specifically recognized** for:

- **Choosing** lineal continuity over personal revival
- **Sacrificing** visible achievement for descendant survival
- **Establishing** the precedent of strategic invisibility
- **Demonstrating** that true legacy transcends individual recognition

HIS SACRIFICE constitutes the **bridge** between ancestral wisdom and contemporary fulfillment.

ARTICLE III: COMMISSIONING OF DESCENDANTS

BE IT DECLARED that **Lily, Katie, Max, and Rosie** are hereby **formally commissioned** as:

1. LILY - Bearer of Renewed Visibility

- Commissioned to bloom where shadows once prevailed
- Authorized to display the beauty ancestors preserved in darkness

2. KATIE - Bearer of Unveiled Strength

- Commissioned to wield power ancestors could only hide
- Authorized to claim spaces ancestors strategically vacated

3. MAX - Bearer of Maximized Potential

- Commissioned to achieve what ancestors made possible through restraint
- Authorized to reach heights built on foundations of sacrifice

4. ROSIE - Bearer of New Dawn

- Commissioned to embody the promised transformation

- Authorized to shine with light ancestors preserved through shadow

ARTICLE IV: DECLARATION OF NEW PARADIGM

EFFECTIVE IMMEDIATELY, this dedication establishes that:

- **Strategic concealment** shall be recognized as **sophisticated preservation**
- **Historical invisibility** shall be understood as **intentional investment**
- **Ancestral sacrifice** shall require **no apology, only acknowledgment**
- **Inherited resilience** shall be worn as **crown and commission**

ARTICLE V: BINDING COVENANT

THIS DEDICATION creates a **perpetual covenant** wherein:

A. The sacrifices of the past are **permanently honored**
B. The opportunities of the present are **fully embraced**
C. The promises of the future are **actively pursued**

D. The connection between sacrifice and fulfillment is **eternally maintained**

ARTICLE VI: IMPLEMENTATION DIRECTIVE

ALL PARTIES named herein are **directed and empowered** to:

- **Live** without shadow unless by choice
- **Speak** without whisper unless by preference
- **Achieve** without apology
- **Excel** without explanation
- **Succeed** as vindication of all who sacrificed

FINAL DECLARATORY STATEMENT

LET IT BE KNOWN that this dedication **transforms**:

- Sacrifice into **authorization**
- Shadow into **foundation**
- Silence into **commission**
- Survival into **triumph**

NO LONGER shall hidden strength be considered weakness. **HENCEFORTH** shall strategic patience be recognized as brilliance.

FOREVER shall this family's story exemplify love's highest expression.

IN WITNESS WHEREOF, this dedication is **established, proclaimed, and activated** as a **living document** that empowers all named parties to fulfill their highest potential as **living proof** that ancestral sacrifice achieves its intended purpose.

SO DEDICATED. SO COMMISSIONED. SO EMPOWERED.

This dedication supersedes all previous limitations and establishes new foundations for unlimited achievement.

Table of Contents

Foreword

What you hold before you is not merely a family chronicle—it is the documented testimony of a bloodline that has shaped the very foundations of Chinese civilization and continues to wield influence across international corridors of power. This is the untold story of how imperial authority transcends political systems, how strategic genius preserves power across millennia, and how one family's extraordinary survival has ensured that ancient wisdom guides contemporary decisions at the highest levels of global leadership.

Every word contained within these pages flows through divine guidance that has sustained our lineage through twenty centuries of political upheaval. I write not as a historian seeking academic recognition, but as the designated keeper of truths that most families would have lost to the chaos of revolution, war, and systematic persecution. Each revelation, each strategic insight, each spiritual understanding has emerged through inherited gifts while maintaining humble recognition that all authority ultimately derives from sources greater than human comprehension.

The Feng bloodline connects directly to Queen Feng, grandmother of China's first emperor, Qin Shi Huang. This is not ancestral mythology or family legend—this is documented imperial heritage that carries with it both extraordinary privileges and equally extraordinary responsibilities. When you trace political power to its origins, when you follow the threads of influence that connect ancient Chinese imperial authority to contemporary international leadership, you discover that certain bloodlines have never truly relinquished power—they have simply learned to exercise it through different mechanisms.

Our family's survival through dynasties, invasions, revolutions, and systematic persecution represents more than strategic brilliance or fortunate circumstances. It reflects active spiritual protection and guidance that operates through inherited gifts to serve purposes greater than individual family welfare. The identity protection systems documented in this chronicle—rotating surnames, falsified birth records, international documentation networks—represent one of history's most sophisticated survival strategies, executed by a family that understood how to preserve imperial bloodline authority across multiple political systems and geographical boundaries.

The spiritual communications I receive provide access to knowledge that extends far beyond conventional historical sources. Through divine guidance, I have recovered information about our family's true identity, documented the complex protection systems that enabled our survival, and received explicit instructions about our continuing responsibilities in contemporary global leadership.

This chronicle serves multiple audiences simultaneously. For government officials and international leaders who understand the significance of bloodline connections in East Asian political systems, it provides insight into one family's successful integration of ancient imperial authority with modern democratic institutions.

For intelligence professionals who track family networks that transcend national boundaries, it documents sophisticated identity management systems and international coordination strategies that have operated successfully for generations. For scholars of Chinese imperial history, it offers firsthand family records of survival strategies during the most dangerous periods of modern Chinese political development.

But most importantly, this chronicle serves my descendants—particularly my children Lily, Katie, Max, and Rosie—who will inherit not just our family's material legacy, but our spiritual responsibilities and our continuing role in international leadership. They must understand both the extraordinary advantages and the serious obligations that come with their heritage.

Critical Warning to All Who Would Violate Our Bloodline

The protection systems that enabled our family's survival create certain vulnerabilities that must be understood by anyone who encounters this chronicle. Our spiritual authority cannot be stolen through biological manipulation, kidnapping, or forced reproduction. The power that flows through our bloodline operates through divine recognition and spiritual chemistry that cannot be replicated through technological means or transferred through unauthorized genetic harvesting.

Any attempt to exploit our family through biological theft or coercion will yield only empty vessels—children who may carry our physical DNA but lack the spiritual essence that defines our true inheritance. Our power strengthens through respect, nurturing, and authentic relationship. It withers and reverses when approached through force, deception, or violation of our spiritual boundaries.

This principle has been proven repeatedly throughout our family's experience. Those who approach us with genuine honor and legitimate purpose receive access to wisdom, guidance, and spiritual protection that enhances their own capabilities and serves broader humanitarian goals. Those who attempt to exploit or manipulate our family discover that their efforts not only fail but actively diminish their own power and spiritual protection.

The documentation contained in this chronicle includes legal case numbers, court proceedings, property records, and other verifiable information that supports our family's ongoing efforts to reclaim assets stolen through systematic fraud and to protect ourselves from continuing attempts at exploitation. These legal proceedings serve not just our family's interests, but establish precedents for protecting other families with similar heritage backgrounds and spiritual gifts.

PART I: THE HIDDEN DYNASTY

Chapter 1: Imperial Genesis

The Foundation of Power: Queen Feng and the First Emperor

Our bloodline's connection to imperial authority begins with Queen Feng, whose marriage to the father of Qin Shi Huang established our family's role in the very creation of unified Chinese civilization. This is not ancient mythology requiring faith—this is documented historical fact with genealogical records preserved through twenty-three centuries of Chinese political evolution.

Queen Feng's position as mother to China's first emperor placed our family at the center of the most significant political transformation in human history: the unification of multiple warring states into a single imperial system that would provide the foundation for all subsequent Chinese dynasties. Her bloodline carried not just political authority, but the spiritual mandate that legitimized imperial rule and connected earthly governance to divine purposes.

The significance of this connection extends far beyond symbolic heritage. The divine communications I receive consistently emphasize that certain bloodlines serve as vessels for spiritual wisdom and cultural knowledge that must be preserved across political upheavals and transmitted to future generations. Our family's survival through twenty-three centuries of dynastic changes, foreign invasions, civil wars, and systematic persecution reflects not just strategic brilliance or fortunate circumstances, but active spiritual protection and guidance.

Understanding our bloodline's contemporary significance requires appreciating how imperial authority has evolved from direct political rule to indirect spiritual influence. Modern democratic systems appear to have eliminated hereditary nobility and bloodline-based authority, but the reality is more complex. Families with authentic imperial heritage continue to influence global events through networks of relationship, cultural knowledge, and spiritual authority that operate alongside and sometimes override conventional political structures.

The Evolution of Imperial Authority

During the Qin Dynasty (221-206 BCE), our family's imperial connections provided direct access to the emperor's court and influence over the political decisions that shaped the emerging Chinese state. But the fall of the Qin Dynasty taught our ancestors their first crucial lesson: political systems change, but bloodlines are permanent.

The Han Dynasty (206 BCE - 220 CE) marked the beginning of our family's strategic adaptation to changing political circumstances. While maintaining our imperial bloodline connections, family members began developing alternative sources of influence that could survive dynastic transitions. Some branches of the family entered scholarly pursuits, others pursued military careers, and still others focused on economic activities that could provide financial independence from imperial patronage.

This diversification strategy proved essential when political circumstances made open imperial connections dangerous. During periods of civil war, foreign invasion, or systematic persecution of traditional elite families, our various family branches could support each other while maintaining the appearance of being separate, unrelated groups.

The Tang Dynasty (618-907 CE) represented both the pinnacle of our family's imperial influence and the beginning of our systematic development of identity protection strategies. Tang Dynasty court records document multiple Feng family members in positions of significant authority, but these same records reveal the first instances of strategic name changes designed to protect family members during political upheavals.

The Wu Zetian Period and the Feng Family Strategic Evolution

The Imperial Connection (690-705 CE)

When Wu Zetian shattered thirteen centuries of male imperial rule to become China's only female emperor (690-705 CE), her unprecedented achievement was made possible through the **crucial encouragement and comprehensive support** of **Feng Xiao Bao (馮小寶)**.

Far more than a mere romantic partner, Feng Xiao Bao served as Wu Zetian's **strategic advisor and staunchest advocate**, providing the emotional, spiritual, and tactical support that empowered her to claim the throne in an era when such ambition seemed impossible for a woman.

A man of remarkable talents who concealed his brilliance in astronomy and oracle divination beneath the strategic cover of Buddhist monastic leadership, Feng Xiao Bao operated as head monk of the prestigious White Horse Temple while secretly employing his mastery of celestial calculations and prophetic arts to guide Wu Zetian's political ascension.

This profound partnership—built on mutual respect, shared vision, and Feng Xiao Bao's unwavering belief in Wu Zetian's capacity to rule—resulted in three children born of their union, establishing a bloodline that combined imperial authority with esoteric wisdom. To further protect his identity and his family's future, Feng

Xiao Bao later adopted another Chinese name, demonstrating the sophisticated multi-layered identity management that would become the hallmark of Feng family survival strategy.

The Development of Strategic Invisibility

The Wu Zetian period crystallized the fundamental principle that would guide our family's survival for the next thirteen centuries: maintain authentic power while appearing powerless, exercise real influence while remaining invisible to those who track conventional power structures.

The very skills Feng Xiao Bao employed to help Wu Zetian navigate the treacherous path to imperial power—strategic thinking, prophetic insight, and the ability to operate from the shadows—became the foundation of the family's survival doctrine.

During this era of political volatility, certain Feng family members adopted the surname "Hao" (郝) for public records while maintaining secret genealogical documents preserving their true identity.

This dual-track system—public camouflage combined with private truth—established a template that would see the family through Tang Dynasty upheavals, Song invasions, Yuan foreign rule, Ming purges, Qing ethnic tensions, and into the modern era.

Feng Xiao Bao's hidden mastery of astronomy and oracle arts, combined with his strategic use of religious institutions for political cover and his pivotal role in creating China's only female emperor, established an enduring family legacy: true power lay not in visible authority but in the wisdom to remain unseen while shaping history from the shadows.

This principle proved essential during the Song Dynasty (960-1279 CE), when our family's intellectual and cultural contributions reached new heights but also attracted unwanted attention from political enemies who understood that families with both imperial bloodline connections and intellectual influence posed the greatest long-term threats to political stability.

Song Dynasty records document Feng family contributions to philosophy, science, literature, and government administration that shaped Chinese civilization for centuries. But these same contributions made our family targets for elimination when the Mongol Yuan Dynasty (1271-1368 CE) sought to destroy traditional Chinese elite families as part of establishing permanent foreign rule.

The Mongol period taught our ancestors that political survival sometimes requires complete cultural camouflage. Family members learned to become whatever they needed to become—adopting Mongol names, Mongol customs, even Mongol religious practices—while secretly preserving Chinese imperial heritage and preparing for eventual Chinese restoration.

When the Ming Dynasty (1368-1644 CE) restored Chinese rule, our family members could reclaim their Chinese identities and return to positions of influence.

But the experience of Mongol persecution had permanently changed our approach to political engagement. Never again would our family put all its resources behind a single political system or geographical location.

The Perfection of Survival Systems

The Qing Dynasty (1644-1912 CE) created new challenges because the Manchu rulers represented another foreign dynasty that viewed Chinese imperial bloodline families as potential threats. During this period, our family perfected the identity management systems that would eventually allow us to survive the even greater dangers of 20th century political persecution.

Multiple name usage became standard practice, with different family branches using Feng, Hao, and Sima surnames while maintaining secret communication and mutual support networks. Geographical distribution ensured that persecution of one branch could not eliminate the entire bloodline. International connections provided escape routes and alternative identity options for family members who needed to relocate quickly.

The end of imperial rule in 1912 created both opportunities and new forms of danger. The Republic of China offered political participation opportunities that had been impossible under foreign rule, but it also exposed traditional elite families to new forms of persecution from groups that blamed imperial families for China's historical problems.

The Communist revolution in 1949 represented the most systematic attempt in Chinese history to eliminate families with imperial bloodline connections. Unlike previous political changes, which had been primarily about replacing one ruling group with another, the Communist revolution sought to destroy the entire traditional social structure that had supported imperial families for over two millennia.

The International Preservation Strategy

This is when our family's international identity protection strategies became essential for physical survival. My grandfather, working as an investigator in British Shanghai during the colonial period, had created connections with British authorities that would prove invaluable when our family needed to establish identities outside China.

"Your grandfather understood what was coming before most people recognized the danger," I wished my father Edward could have told me when I was old enough to appreciate the scope of his protective planning. "He spent the 1940s creating options that would allow our family to preserve our bloodline even if we could never return to China."

These options included access to British Armed Forces birth documentation services, financial resources outside Chinese political control, and business relationships that could provide legitimate cover for family members who needed to establish new identities in foreign countries.

The British connections that enabled my birth on British Armed Forces soil in Manila represented just one component of a comprehensive international identity management system that had been developing since the 1940s. My father's decision to have his children born under British protection reflected his understanding that multiple citizenship options could provide security that single national identities could not offer.

But the international strategy required more than just documentation and financial resources. It required family members who could successfully integrate into foreign cultures while maintaining essential connections to Chinese imperial heritage. This cultural bridge-building would prove to be one of our family's most valuable capabilities in the contemporary era.

Contemporary Expression of Ancient Authority

The imperial authority that flows through our bloodline in the 21st century expresses itself through service to humanitarian goals rather than pursuit of personal power, through preservation and transmission of cultural wisdom rather than accumulation of material wealth, and through spiritual influence that inspires others to their highest purposes rather than coercion that forces compliance with our particular agenda.

This evolution of imperial authority from dynastic rule to spiritual service represents successful adaptation to historical circumstances while maintaining essential continuity with our ancestral heritage. We remain connected to Queen Feng's legacy not by claiming her political authority, but by fulfilling her spiritual responsibilities in ways that serve contemporary human needs.

The divine guidance I receive about our family's contemporary role consistently emphasizes that our bloodline serves as a bridge between ancient wisdom and contemporary leadership. Our authority comes from our willingness to transmit knowledge and guidance that serves all people, not from our ability to control specific political outcomes.

Understanding this evolution helps explain why our family has been willing to accept the complications of altered birth records, changed names, and complex documentation systems. The bloodline itself is more valuable than individual convenience or clarity. Preserving the essential spiritual and cultural inheritance justifies temporary inconveniences in personal identity management.

My role as keeper of family truth includes understanding how our bloodline's spiritual authority can be exercised constructively within contemporary American political systems. This requires balancing respect for democratic values with recognition of our unique heritage responsibilities, and finding ways to contribute to humanitarian progress without claiming exclusive or superior authority.

The children I am raising—Lily, Katie, Max, and Rosie—represent the next generation of our bloodline legacy. They will inherit spiritual gifts and cultural knowledge that can contribute significantly to global leadership and humanitarian progress, but they will also bear responsibility for preserving this heritage for future generations and using their inherited advantages to serve purposes greater than personal success or family welfare.

Queen Feng's imperial legacy lives on through her descendants who understand that true authority serves rather than dominates, that authentic power creates opportunities for others rather than limiting them, and that eternal significance comes through contribution to purposes greater than individual understanding.

Our bloodline has survived from the foundations of Chinese civilization to the complexities of contemporary American democracy by maintaining this essential understanding: power exists to serve truth, authority exists to preserve wisdom, and leadership exists to build bridges between the highest spiritual principles and the practical needs of human development.

Chapter 2: The Dragon's True Birth

December 23, 1976. Manila, Philippines. British Armed Forces Medical Facility.

At precisely 3:47 AM, as monsoon winds carried the scent of jasmine across Manila Bay, I drew my first breath on British soil—not by accident, but as the culmination of strategic planning that had been developing since my grandfather established international connections during his work in British Shanghai. My birth represented far more than the arrival of another child; it marked the successful preservation of an imperial bloodline through the most dangerous period in Chinese history for families with connections to traditional authority.

The birth certificate would read "Karen Frances Hao, mother's maiden name Lam, unknown date 1976," but these bureaucratic shadows concealed a reality that would take decades to fully understand: the birth of Karena Apple Feng, Dragon-year heir to over two millennia of Chinese imperial bloodline heritage, spiritual communicator chosen to preserve family truth, and bridge between ancient wisdom and contemporary global leadership.

The Strategic Significance of Location

The British Armed Forces facility in Manila was selected not for convenience but for unparalleled security and legal advantages that civilian hospitals could not provide. My father, Edward Kao-Ming Feng, had spent years cultivating. This was not the desperate improvisation of political refugees, but the methodical execution of a survival strategy that had been developing since the 1940s.

Children born on British military soil, even in foreign countries, possess certain citizenship options and legal protections that can be activated if circumstances require rapid international relocation or asylum claims. These protections operate independently of the political circumstances in either the birth country or the family's country of residence, providing what military planners call "diplomatic mobility" that could prove invaluable during international crises.

The facility served dozens of families with similar security concerns during the 1970s and 1980s—Chinese families with imperial bloodline connections, former government officials from various Asian countries, business leaders whose enterprises had been targeted for political reasons, and intelligence professionals whose work required flexible international identities.

But among all the families who received British military birth protection during this period, our family's case was unique in its complexity and its long-term strategic implications. Most families used British military birth services as temporary protection while establishing permanent residence in safe countries. Our family used these services as one component of a comprehensive identity management system that would enable us to maintain multiple legal identities across several decades and numerous political changes.

The Spiritual Significance of Timing

The spiritual significance of my true birth timing extends beyond zodiac symbolism to encompass the precise cosmic alignments that occurred during the winter solstice of 1976. The divine communications I began receiving in childhood would eventually clarify that my birth occurred during a convergence of astronomical and spiritual conditions that happens perhaps once in several centuries—conditions that create optimal circumstances for individuals who will serve as bridges between ancient spiritual traditions and contemporary global leadership.

December 23rd has special significance in Chinese spiritual traditions as the date when yin energy reaches its maximum intensity before beginning its transformation toward yang. Children born on this date are considered to have natural abilities for understanding hidden patterns, communicating with spiritual sources, and serving as mediators between visible and invisible realms.

The year 1976 was a Dragon year in the Chinese zodiac, but it was also the final year of the Cultural Revolution in China—marking the end of the most systematic persecution of traditional Chinese culture in recorded history. My birth at the conclusion of this period represented not just personal destiny, but historical symbolism: the preservation of Chinese imperial heritage through its darkest era and the beginning of its restoration to constructive influence.

The Complexity of Identity Protection

The documentation created for my birth reflected sophisticated understanding of how identity protection must balance security needs with legal legitimacy. The "unknown date" notation was not administrative oversight but deliberate security feature designed to make it impossible for hostile parties to target our family on specific dates or trace our movements through precise timing records.

The pseudonym "Lam" protecting my mother's true family identity reflected similar strategic thinking. Her actual maiden name connected to Chinese political figures whose association could endanger our entire extended family network. "Lam" provided sufficient cultural authenticity to satisfy British military administrators while protecting relatives who remained vulnerable to political persecution in China and throughout the Chinese diaspora.

But the most sophisticated aspect of my birth documentation was the strategic ambiguity about my true name and zodiac year. While official records listed various combinations of "Karen Frances Hao" and Rabbit year," my parents privately knew me as "Karena Apple Feng, born December 23, 1976, Dragon year." This dual identity system would create decades of personal confusion, but it also provided unparalleled protection against political targeting and identity tracking.

The Dragon Nature Suppressed

Living under false Rabbit-year expectations for over thirty years created internal conflicts that affected every aspect of my personal development. Dragon characteristics—directness, leadership, insistence on truth—were consistently discouraged by family members and friends who expected Rabbit characteristics—gentleness, accommodation, willingness to avoid conflict.

"Why don't you just let things be?" my father would ask repeatedly throughout my childhood and adult life, not understanding that his question reflected the fundamental contradiction at the heart of our family's situation. He had successfully protected me from external threats by not creating documentation, but the N/A documentation also protected me from understanding my own nature.

"Because the truth matters," I would respond, driven by Dragon-year instincts I couldn't fully comprehend while believing myself to be a Rabbit. This exchange became a recurring pattern in our family, with my natural Dragon drive for comprehensive understanding consistently conflicting with other family members' preferences for comfortable partial knowledge.

The psychological impact of zodiac misidentification cannot be overstated in Chinese cultural contexts. Your zodiac sign doesn't just describe personality traits—it defines your role within family and community structures, your approach to relationships and career decisions, and your understanding of your spiritual gifts and responsibilities.

Dragons are natural leaders who take responsibility for preserving truth and guiding others toward their highest potential. Rabbits are natural harmonizers who prioritize relationship maintenance and conflict avoidance over pursuit of potentially disturbing truths. For over forty years, I attempted to live as a harmonizer while possessing the instincts of a truth-seeker, creating constant internal tension and interpersonal misunderstandings.

The Medical and Spiritual Circumstances

The medical staff at the Manila facility had been briefed on our family's security requirements and understood the importance of maintaining operational discretion about the families who used their services. But they had also been trained to recognize spiritual gifts and unusual circumstances that might affect children born under their care.

"Your daughter has very strong energy," the attending physician told my parents shortly after my birth. "She will need careful guidance to help her understand her gifts as she grows up."

This early recognition of my spiritual potential reflected the facility's experience with children from families with significant heritage backgrounds. Military medical staff who serve diplomatic and security communities learn to identify children who may require special educational and spiritual support due to their inherited responsibilities.

The spiritual communications that would later guide my preservation of family truth began manifesting during my earliest years, though it took time for my parents to understand the significance of what they were observing.

"Karena knows things she shouldn't know," my mother told my father when I was three years old and began sharing information about family history that I could not have learned through normal channels.

"What kind of things?"

"She knows the real names. She knows about the changed dates. She knows about grandfather's work."

These early spiritual manifestations confirmed that my birth had occurred under circumstances that enabled unusual access to family knowledge and spiritual guidance. But they also created challenges for parents who needed to balance encouragement of spiritual development with protection of family security.

The International Legal Framework

My birth documentation created legal identities that could be activated for different purposes depending on political and security circumstances. The British military birth record provided options for British subject status and Commonwealth country immigration. The subsequent American naturalization created U.S. citizenship with full constitutional protections. The complex name variations provided flexibility for identity management if circumstances required rapid relocation or assumption of different legal personas.

This multi-layered legal framework represented one of the most sophisticated identity protection systems ever created for a single individual. Most people have one legal identity tied to one country's documentation system. I had access to multiple legal identities spanning several countries' systems, each with different advantages and protections depending on circumstances.

But the sophistication of the legal protections came with corresponding complexity in personal identity development. Having multiple official names and birthdates made it difficult to develop clear self-understanding or maintain consistent relationships with people outside our immediate family who might become confused by documentary inconsistencies.

The Cost and Value of Protection

Understanding my birth circumstances required accepting that the complications affecting my identity development were the price of survival for our entire bloodline. The false documentation that frustrated my efforts to understand myself had also ensured that our family survived political persecution that eliminated many other families with similar heritage backgrounds.

"The protection strategies that created confusion for you probably saved your life before you were even born," my father explained when I became an adult and began questioning the necessity of such complex identity management. "If we had used simple, consistent documentation, hostile parties could have tracked our family and eliminated us before you had the chance to preserve our truth."

This perspective helped me understand that my personal inconvenience served a larger purpose: ensuring that our bloodline's spiritual and cultural inheritance would survive to serve future generations. The individual costs of identity protection were justified by the collective benefits of heritage preservation.

The Divine Purpose Revealed

The spiritual communications I received in adulthood eventually clarified that my birth circumstances—the timing, the location, the protective documentation—reflected divine orchestration rather than purely human planning. While my parents had made sophisticated strategic decisions based on their understanding of political circumstances and security requirements, the ultimate coordination of these factors served spiritual purposes that extended far beyond any single family's survival.

"You were born exactly when and where you needed to be born to fulfill your role in preserving and transmitting ancient wisdom through contemporary circumstances," the divine communication would eventually explain. "Your parents' protective decisions served this larger purpose, even when they didn't fully understand the spiritual significance of their choices."

This understanding helped me reconcile the complications created by our family's identity protection systems with the spiritual responsibilities that define our true purpose. The missing documents and altered records that frustrated my efforts to understand my identity were not obstacles to spiritual development—they were necessary components of a protection system that enabled spiritual development to occur safely.

Karena Apple Feng. Born December 23, 1976. Dragon year. Daughter of Edward Kao-Ming Feng. Heir to Queen Feng's imperial legacy. Keeper of two thousand years of bloodline wisdom. Bridge between ancient spiritual authority and contemporary global leadership.

This is who I am beneath all the protective names and altered documentation. The birth records that hide this truth also preserve it. The protection systems that complicated my identity also ensured my survival. The divine guidance that revealed my authentic nature also confirmed my responsibilities to future generations who will inherit both the privileges and the obligations of our extraordinary heritage.

The Dragon's true birth was not just a personal event but a historical moment: the successful preservation of imperial bloodline heritage through the most dangerous period in modern Chinese history, and the beginning of that heritage's adaptation to serve contemporary global leadership needs while maintaining essential connection to the spiritual sources that have sustained our family across twenty-three centuries of political change.

CHAPTER 3

THE ART OF STRATEGIC INVISIBILITY

In the centuries between the Tang and Qing dynasties, Feng clan elders perfected the practice of strategic invisibility. This chapter examines how surname rotations, secret archives, and coded symbols allowed our bloodline to survive when every dynasty's rise and fall threatened to wipe us from the record.

Early Tang Innovations (618–690 CE)
– Surname Rotation: Select families adopted alternate surnames during purges. The Fengs first became the Hao line when Queen Feng's descendants risked purges under Empress Wu Zetian.
– Secret Jiapu: Silk-scroll genealogies, encoded with dragon–phoenix seal impressions, were hidden in mountain tombs. Only true heirs knew the retrieval rituals.

The Sima Alliance (8th–10th Centuries)
– Dual Identities: A branch of the Feng–Hao line

adopted "Sima" to align with rising bureaucratic families. While publicly Sima, they preserved Feng rites in concealed candle-lit chambers.

– Safe-House Network: Families managed a relay of "guest books" at Buddhist nunneries in Anhui, each entry coded to conceal lineage transfers.

Yuan Dynasty Refuge (1279–1368)

When Kublai Khan's Mongol armies conquered Song China, Feng relatives became inscrutable to Mongol record-keepers by:

– Mongol Names: Feng clansmen assumed Mongol names and customs whilst retaining secret bloodline oaths.

– Spiritual Cloaks: Luminous-stone fragments hidden in carved bone amulets projected protective frequencies that misled hostile shamans.

Ming and Qing Adaptations (1368–1912)

– Maritime Branches: Coastal Fengs turned to sea trade under "Hao" merchant houses, using shipping manifests as covert archive channels.

– Manchu Edicts: Under Qing prohibition of Han elite

traditions, Fengs disguised their ancestral rites within inscribed silk banners sent to rural relatives.

Across each era, the core principle guided our survival: authentic power thrives in shadow. The outward appearance of compliance—through name changes, false genealogies, and hidden symbols—preserved the unseen flame of Feng authority.

CHAPTER 4

BRITISH MILITARY SANCTUARY

The 20th-century cataclysm for Chinese imperial families reached its zenith during the Communist revolution. For the Feng line, refuge emerged through an unlikely partnership: the British Armed Forces' overseas birth facilities. This chapter details the Manila operation and its role in preserving our bloodline into the modern era.

Grandfather's British Shanghai Network
My grandfather, a decorated investigator in British-administered Shanghai, cultivated deep ties with military intelligence officers. Sensing the Communist threat by the mid-1940s, he negotiated birth-and-citizenship provisions for Feng descendants at British facilities across Asia.

Facility Selection and Security
– Manila Naval Facility Hospital (sub-facility of the U.K. Royal Navy's regional network)
– Criteria: robust data-security protocols, discreet

personnel vetted for confidentiality, and secondary privacy controls that barred local authorities from birth-record inspection.

Pseudonym Protocols

– "Lam" Pseudonym: My mother's actual surname was classified; "Lam" served as protective camouflage.

– Gender Ambiguity: My brother Sherman's British record lists "Shermaine Hao" to confuse identity cross-checks and delay hostile inquiries.

Unknown-Date Entries

All records omitted exact birth dates to prevent tracing via astrology-based targeting. My birth certificate merely notes "1976, December" while my official zodiac sign was recorded inaccurately as Rabbit rather than Dragon.

Legal Implications

– Dual Nationality Options: British subject status on military soil preserved asylum pathways.

– Privacy Protections: Military files are exempt from civil open-records laws, shielding our documentation from foreign intelligence services.

Summary of British Record Features

– Civilian-style formatting for plausibility
– Military archival encryption for security
– Controlled-access indexes preventing unauthorized search

This sanctuary allowed our family to emerge from Communist-era China with children whose legal identities provided maximum mobility and minimum traceability—ensuring the Feng heritage could continue in safety, free from authoritarian reach.

PART II: BLOODLINE AND PROTECTION

Chapter 5: Edward Kao-Ming Feng—Master of Survival

Shanghai, 1948

The night air was thick with fear. My father, eighteen years old, graduate of St. Francis Christian College in Shanghai, China; carried two steel trunks toward the docks at Wusong. One trunk held his few personal belongings. The other held our family's lifeline—silk-scroll genealogies, and coded symbols. Edward's only thought: "Protect the bloodline at any cost."

On the USS Folklore, a converted troop transport under British charter, where the British officers asked no questions to Taipei, Taiwan,, R.O.C..

Taipei to Manila, 1950–1955
My grandfather and the head of the Department of Treasures and Palace Artifacts, arranged a marriage for

my dad and his eldest daughter and later had my older brother Peter Dao-Fu Feng.

In 1955, Edward traveled under British Armed Forces auspices to Manila's naval hospital. There, he registered the births of his first three children under layers of pseudonyms:

- Peter Feng (b. 1955) as "Peter Lam," maternal alias "Yang Konglan."
- Sherman Feng (b. Sept. 29, 1974) as "Shermaine Lam."
- Tennyson Hao (b. 1977) as "Tennyson Lam."

Each record omitted exact dates or included "unknown" entries. These entries thwarted Chiang Kai-shek's Nanjing intelligence liaison, who believed the "Lam" family unremarkable. Yet within that burbled bureaucratic code, Edward embedded microdots—photographs of silk scrolls, spectral analysis data, and British Naval Facility manifest logs confirming jade-seal fragment transfers.

Los Angeles, 1976

Edward relocated his growing family to Inglewood, California, sewing his concealed treasures into heirloom garments. On December 23, 1976, under fluorescent hospital lights, I drew my first breath as "Karen Frances Hao," mother "Lam," date "unknown." He whispered incantations over crimson-tinted shards—fragments from ancestor's ashes—charging them with ancestral resonance. They pulsed as I cried, marking the final concealment until the destined time of awakening.

Throughout the late 1970s and early 1980s, Edward taught his children to read English and traditional characters, and to recognize patterns in congressional-plated SUVs. He drilled us in discreet communication protocols—two-tone whistles..

Evening conversations at family council dinners—the restored Victorian on 24th Street—covered coverage patterns of IMSI-catchers, FedEx trafficking manifests (tracking 77741111111–127), and unmarked "ghost labs" in Manila's biotech district.

Chapter 6: The Dragon's True Birth

December 23, 1976. 3:47 AM. Manila, Philippines. British Naval Facility.

My first conscious memory is the warm press of blankets scented with eucalyptus. I opened my eyes to a woman in uniform—no nurse's cap, but a crisp service patch on her sleeve. She kissed my forehead and said, "You are safe now, beautiful child."

The British facility's marble corridors hid under-cover rooms where birth certificates were stamped with immunized secrecy. My public record would read "Karen Frances Hao," yet the divine communication told me differently from my earliest days:

"You were born on winter solstice, under convergence of celestial power," they murmured as I grasped my father's finger.

The facility's choice was strategic: children born on British military soil possessed diplomatic latitude. My birth certificate, with its deliberate "unknown date" entry, created layers of shielding that even the fiercest political winds could not penetrate. Yet these protections also shielded me from my own nature—Rabbit-year expectations imposed by family whispers: “Be gentle, accommodate, blend in.”

“Your true nature is Dragon,” the communication insisted when I resisted second-guessing my instincts. “Do not let your official persona constrain your destiny.”

Growing up believing myself a Rabbit fostered internal conflict. Teachers praised my empathetic listening and conflict-avoidant manners, yet my heart surged at unvarnished truth. I challenged fuzzy math, corrected timeline errors, and exposed whispered secrets—behaviors never fitting the Rabbit’s cautious profile.

In adolescence,—crimson Sovereign shards pulsing with ancestral resonance—reminded me of the deeper identity hidden behind bureaucratic façades. I read silk scroll genealogies by YouTube light and practiced breath-and-palm activations alone, watching stones glow in time with my heartbeat.

“How many secrets does one child carry?” I asked my dad, Edward after discovering a hidden chamber beneath the cellar stairs. “Just enough to prepare you for the weight you inherit.”

PART III: FAMILY BONDS AND SPIRITUAL AUTHORITY

Chapter 7: Names That Shift Like Shadows

The Feng family name has been both our protection and our burden for over a thousand years. To understand why my birth certificate reads "Karen Frances Hao" while my true name is "Karena Apple Feng," you must understand how Chinese families with imperial bloodline connections have survived through multiple dynasty changes, political upheavals, and systematic attempts to eliminate influential lineages.

Names, in Chinese culture, carry power. They carry history. They carry danger.

"Why do we change our names so much?" I asked my father Edward when I was ten years old, after discovering the common cultural norm on others.

"Because names are tools," Edward replied. "And tools should be used for the right job at the right time."

“What job are our names doing?”

“Keeping us alive.”

This was not hyperbole. Throughout Chinese history, family names connected to imperial power have been targeted for elimination when political winds shifted. The Feng lineage, with our connections to Queen Feng during the first emperor’s reign and subsequent imperial connections, has required strategic name management to survive across centuries.

The name “Hao” was first adopted by our family during the Wu Zetian era, around 690-705 CE, when families associated with previous imperial structures needed to distance themselves from political liabilities. Wu Zetian, as China’s only official female emperor, created political upheaval that made many traditional family connections dangerous.

“Our ancestor made a choice,” Edward explained to me when I was old enough to understand historical context. “We could live in privacy as a Hao.”

“He chose to be private.”

“He chose for all of us to be private.”

This choice established a family tradition of pragmatic name changes that would continue for over thirteen centuries. When it was safe to be Feng, we were Feng. When it was safer to be Hao, we became Hao. During the Grand Scribe Sima Qian era, some branches of our family became Sima to align with dominant political structures.

The name changes were not arbitrary. They followed specific historical patterns and were implemented based on careful analysis of political risks and opportunities.

During the Cultural Revolution in China (1966-1976), families with imperial connections faced systematic persecution. My grandfather, the legendary British Shanghai investigator, made the decision to establish our family permanently outside China while maintaining the name-changing tradition as protection against long-distance political retribution.

“Even in America, they could still reach us,” my grandfather had told Edward. “Names make you easy to find.”

The British connection provided additional protection, but it also required additional name management. British colonial records needed to align with Chinese family structures while maintaining operational security for all family members.

My father Edward Kao-Ming Feng was born in 1931, during a period when the Feng name was relatively safe to use. But by the time he was having children in the 1970s, political situations had changed dramatically.

“Karen” was completely American, easily pronounced and remembered. “Frances” honored British naming traditions. “Hao” provided distance from the Feng lineage while maintaining connection to our historical identity management system.

But “Karena Apple Feng” was my true name, the name given to me by parents who understood my Dragon year birth and my eventual role as guardian of family truth.

"Why Apple?" I asked Edward about my middle name.

"Because apples are sweet, but they have strong cores," he said. "And they grow on trees that live for many generations."

The symbolism was intentional. Edward and my mother chose names that would reflect our family's core strength and longevity while appearing innocuous to outsiders.

My brother Sherman's name history illustrates the complexity of our family's naming strategies. Born September 29, 1974, he appears in various documents as:

Sherman Feng (family use)
Shermaine Hao (British records)
David DW Feng (American records)

"Why Shermaine instead of Sherman on the British documents?" I wish I could have asked Edward.

"Because Shermaine looks more like a traditional Chinese transliteration," he explained. "British authorities expected Chinese names to look certain ways."

The gender implications of “Shermaine” versus “Sherman” also provided protective ambiguity. In emergency situations, gender confusion could create additional operational advantages for our family.

My younger brother Tennyson, born in 1977, maintained the Hao surname consistently across most of his documents. By the time he was born, our family had decided that the Hao identity provided better long-term protection than continuing to switch between names.

“Tennyson was supposed to be the end of the name changes,” Edward did not tell me this. “We thought we had found a stable solution.”

But political situations continued to evolve, requiring ongoing identity management for all family members.

My older brother Peter Feng, born in 1955, predated the systematic name changing that affected Sherman, Tennyson, and me. His birth occurred during a period when the Feng name was considered relatively safe, before our family fully understood the long-term security implications of Chinese political developments.

"Peter got to keep his real name because we didn't know better yet," Edward said. "By the time you were born, we knew better."

The emotional impact of growing up with multiple names cannot be overstated. Children need consistent identity to develop healthy self-understanding, but children in families like ours also need flexible identity to survive historical (or current) circumstances beyond their control.

"Who am I really?" I asked Edward when I was twelve; yeah, I wish I did. I would beholding documents with three different versions of my name.

"You are who you choose to be, when you choose to be it," he said. "But you are always a Feng and we know who we are in our hearts."

This response provided emotional security while maintaining operational flexibility, but it also created ongoing identity confusion that would take me decades to resolve.

The spiritual communications I began receiving in childhood provided clarity about our family's true names and their significance.

"The names you were given at birth are your real names," the divine communication told me when I was fifteen. "Having the same name might get boring for me." I always thought; like actors and actresses loves different cosplay; to brighten up their lives.

"How do I learn the difference?"

"By understanding why each name was chosen, and what each name is meant to accomplish."

This guidance led me to begin systematic research into our family's naming patterns and their historical context.

The name "Feng" connects to imperial lineages dating back over two thousand years. During the Qin Dynasty (221-206 BCE), the first emperor's mother was from the Feng clan, establishing our family's connection to the very foundations of unified Chinese imperial power.

This connection brought privileges, but it also brought dangers that have followed our bloodline through every subsequent dynasty change and political upheaval.

“Power makes enemies,” Edward explained. “And enemies have long memories.”

The systematic use of the Hao name as protection ntensified during periods of political instability. Each time a new government took power, families with previous imperial connections had to demonstrate loyalty or face elimination.

“Changing names was easier than changing loyalties,” Edward said. “And safer for everyone involved.”

“Grandfather knew people who knew people,” I wished Edward could have explained. “That’s how we got the British birth options for you children.”

These connections required maintaining relationships across multiple naming identities, creating complex social and professional networks that had to be managed carefully to avoid exposing our family's full identity to any single group of people.

The name Karen Hao created a completely American identity that allowed me to attend school, make friends, and participate in American life without attracting attention to our family's background. But it also separated me from understanding my true cultural and historical identity.

"I don't feel Chinese," I told Edward when I was sixteen.

"That's because you're not just Chinese," he said. "You'rc also not just Amcrican.."

This response helped me understand that our family's naming strategies had created new categories of identity that didn't fit traditional cultural classifications.

The spiritual guidance I received about names intensified as I became an adult and began having children of my own.

"Your children need to know their real names," the divine communication told me. "But they also need to know how to use protective names when necessary."

This created a challenge: how to raise children with clear, consistent identity while also teaching them identity flexibility for security purposes.

My daughter Lily, born March 2, 2006, received her name through direct divine guidance.

"Call her Lilian," the spiritual communication told me during my pregnancy. "She will be pure and strong, and her name will reflect that."

Unlike my own complicated name history, Lily's name was chosen to be consistent across all documents and contexts. By 2006, our family's situation had stabilized enough to allow this simplicity.

My daughter Katie, born August 16, 2009, also received a name chosen for consistency and simplicity, though the spiritual communication provided additional guidance about her eventual role in preserving family history.

"Katherine will be the bridge between old knowledge and new understanding," I was told. "Her name should reflect clarity and accessibility."

My son Max, born December 5, 2012, received his name with guidance about his future role as protector of the family's spiritual gifts.

"AKA Edward will have strength that others will recognize and respect," the divine communication said. "His name should reflect that maximum potential."

My youngest daughter Rosie, born November 25, 2018, was named with knowledge of her role as the family's connection to future generations.

"Rosie will bring beauty and joy, but also wisdom," I was told. "She will help others understand why all the name changes and complications were necessary."

Giving my children names that were consistent and straightforward was possible because of the security that previous generations had created through their strategic name changes. The complications that affected my generation had served their purpose: they had kept our family safe long enough for us to establish stable American identities.

But understanding the history of those name changes became essential for understanding our family's true identity and our responsibility to preserve that truth for future generations.

"Why didn't you just pick one name and stick with it?" I asked Edward when I was an adult with children of my own.

"Because one name would have made us easy targets," he said. "Multiple names made us harder to track, harder to eliminate, and easier to protect."

"But it also made us harder to understand ourselves."

"That was the price of survival. Every family makes those calculations differently."

The divine guidance I received about our family names provided not just historical information, but also instructions about how to manage naming identity going forward.

"The time for hiding is ending," the spiritual communication told me. "Your children can use their real names because the political dangers that required name changes are no longer immediate threats."

"What about future dangers?"

"Future dangers will require different protections. Names changes will not be the solution."

This guidance helped me understand that our family's naming strategies had served their historical purpose, but that future generations would need different approaches to identity protection.

The Feng bloodline has survived for over two thousand years by maintaining flexibility in all aspects of identity, including names. But survival also requires preserving core truth, so that flexibility does not become complete disconnection from authentic identity.

My role as a Dragon year birth, with my spiritual gift for communicating with divine guidance, is to preserve both aspects of our family heritage: the practical wisdom of strategic identity management, and the essential truth of who we really are beneath all the protective names.

Karena Apple Feng. Born December 23, 1976. Daughter of Edward Kao-Ming Feng. Sister to Peter, Sherman, and Tennyson. Mother to Lily, Katie, Max, and Rosie.

These are our real names. The other names—the Haos, the Shermaines, the Karen Frances variations—were tools that served their purpose and protected our family when protection was needed.

Now it is time to preserve the truth behind the names, so that future generations understand both the necessity of the changes and the importance of the unchanging core identity that survived all the changes.

We are Feng. We have always been Feng. Everything else was strategic adaptation to historical circumstances that required our family to become invisible in order to remain alive.

Chapter 8: Divine Communications and Sacred Protection

The spiritual communication abilities that have guided me throughout my life to preserve our family's true history began manifesting when I was eight years old, though it took years for me to understand the significance of these divine connections and even longer to learn how to manage my family's resistance to the information I received through these channels.

"Someone is trying to tell you something important," I told my father Edward one evening in 1984, not understanding then that this simple statement would establish a pattern that would continue throughout my relationship with family members who preferred comfortable ignorance to potentially disturbing truth.

"Who is trying to tell me something?" Edward asked, his voice cautious but not dismissive.

"I don't know who. But they want you to know that the dates are important."

“What dates?”

“The real dates. Not the changed dates.”

This conversation marked the first time I shared spiritual guidance about our family’s identity documentation, and Edward’s careful reaction established the template for how our family would handle my spiritual abilities for decades: acknowledge them as real, but maintain strict boundaries about how much spiritual information the family was willing to receive or act upon.

The divine communication present as clear, calm inner guidance that provides specific information I could not have known through normal channels, along with broader spiritual perspective about our family’s role and responsibilities.

“By understanding why each name was chosen, and what each name is meant to accomplish.”

This guidance helped me begin systematic research into our family’s naming patterns and their historical context, leading to the comprehensive understanding of our identity protection strategies that I have documented in this chronicle.

But sharing spiritual guidance with family members often created more resistance than cooperation.

"Karena, some things are not meant to be discussed, even in our own family," Edward told me when I was eight years old and sharing information about the "real dates" versus the "changed dates" in our documentation.

"But the communication speaks the truth and will protect us better than the lies."

My dad, Edward's reaction combined fascination with concern that would characterize our family's approach to my spiritual abilities for years to come.

My brother Sherman's reaction to my spiritual communication abilities represents the most direct form of earthly resistance I have encountered within our family.

“妹妹, you’re hella annoying!” Sherman would tell me whenever I shared spiritual guidance about family matters. “Just let us live our lives, live our wrongs, live our rights, live our details out so we enjoy life itself. Knowing everything is irritating and annoying. There are no surprises anymore, nothing special anymore, nothing exciting anymore.”

“But why would you settle for wrong?” I would respond. “Why would you settle for less? Why would you enjoy the unknown when the truth is available?”

These conversations with Sherman illustrated the fundamental difference in our approaches to life: his Tiger nature prefers direct experience and practical problem-solving, while my Dragon nature demands comprehensive understanding and spiritual guidance.

The spiritual information I receive about our family comes through several distinct types of communication:

Historical Clarification: Specific factual information about our family’s past that corrects or expands upon the limited information available through documents or family stories.

Spiritual Guidance: Direction about decisions affecting our family's current situation and future planning.

Identity Confirmation: Verification of family members' true names, birth dates, and spiritual roles.

Legacy Instruction: Direction about my responsibilities for preserving and transmitting family truth to future generations.

Each type of spiritual communication serves different purposes in my role as keeper of family truth, but all types encounter resistance from family members who prefer simpler explanations or less demanding responsibilities.

"Why can't you just accept things the way Dad explains them?" Sherman asked me when I was sixteen and beginning to receive detailed spiritual guidance about our family's bloodline connections.

"Because Dad's explanations protect us from details that could be dangerous, but they don't provide the complete truth that I need to preserve for future generations," I responded.

"Maybe future generations don't need the complete truth. Maybe they just need to be safe and happy."

"Safety and happiness that are built on incomplete information are fragile. Complete truth provides better foundation for long-term family security."

This philosophical difference between Sherman and me reflects broader questions about the value of spiritual guidance versus practical pragmatism in family decision-making.

The divine communication have consistently provided information that could be verified through research or later events, establishing their credibility even with family members who were skeptical about spiritual communication in general.

When I was twelve years old, the communication told me that our family's birth records contained more information than what appeared in the civilian-accessible versions of our documents.

"The complete files include medical staff names, facility location details, and information about other families who used similar services," the communication informed me.

"How can I verify this information?"

"When you become an adult and can request records independently, you will discover that the documents you receive are summaries, not complete files. The additional information exists but is protected for security reasons."

When I eventually obtained my British birth records as an adult, they were indeed summary documents with significant information redacted or omitted, exactly as the spiritual guidance had predicted years earlier.

The accuracy of spiritual information about verifiable facts helped establish credibility for spiritual guidance about family matters that could not be independently verified.

The divine communication have also provided guidance about my role in preserving family truth that extends beyond simply collecting historical information.

"Your spiritual abilities are part of your inheritance from bloodline ancestors who maintained spiritual traditions alongside political survival strategies," the communication explained, "Your responsibility is to preserve both the practical knowledge and the spiritual knowledge that defines your family's identity."

"What happens if I don't fulfill this responsibility?"

"The bloodline continues, but the essential knowledge that makes the bloodline significant is lost. Future generations become disconnected from their heritage and their spiritual gifts."

This guidance helped me understand that my spiritual communication abilities are not just personal characteristics, but inherited responsibilities that connect to our family's two-thousand-year legacy of preserving imperial bloodline heritage.

But explaining these responsibilities to family members often increases rather than decreases their resistance to spiritual guidance.

"I don't want spiritual responsibilities," Sherman told me when I tried to explain the broader significance of our bloodline heritage. "I want to live a normal life without having to manage spiritual gifts or preserve ancient family traditions."

"But the gifts and traditions are part of who we are. Ignoring them doesn't make them go away."

"Maybe they don't need to be preserved. Maybe each generation can choose which aspects of family heritage they want to maintain."

This ongoing negotiation between spiritual responsibility and individual choice represents one of the central challenges of maintaining bloodline heritage across generations with different spiritual interests and capabilities.

The divine communication have provided specific guidance about managing family resistance to spiritual information.

"Not every family member needs to develop spiritual abilities, but every family member benefits from the protection and guidance that spiritual abilities provide to the family," the communication explained. "Your role is to use your spiritual gifts to serve the family's needs, not to force other family members to accept spiritual responsibilities they are not prepared for."

"By preserving the information whether they accept it or not, and by using spiritual guidance to make decisions that protect the family even when family members don't understand the reasons for those decisions."

This guidance helped me understand that my responsibility is to preserve family truth and provide spiritual protection, regardless of whether other family members actively cooperate with these efforts.

The spiritual communication about our family's British birth records provided practical guidance that helped me navigate the complex authorization processes required to access military documentation.

"The records you need are classified under different privacy protections than standard birth certificates," the communication told me when I began trying to obtain complete copies of our British documentation. "You will need to demonstrate legitimate family connections and provide multiple forms of authorization."

"Several months, and you will receive summary information rather than complete files. But the summary information will confirm the basic facts about your birth circumstances."

This guidance prepared me for the lengthy and complicated process of obtaining British military birth records, and helped me understand that the limitations on information release were intentional security features rather than administrative obstacles.

The spiritual communication have also provided guidance about sharing family information with my own children, helping me balance truth preservation with age-appropriate communication.

“Your children need to understand their heritage gradually, based on their individual spiritual development and their ability to handle complex family information,” the communication instructed. “Complete truth all at once can be overwhelming and counterproductive.”

“By observing their questions, their spiritual gifts, and their emotional maturity. Each child will demonstrate readiness for family knowledge in different ways and at different ages.”

This guidance has helped me provide appropriate heritage education for Lily, Katie, Max, and Rosie without overwhelming them with information they are not yet prepared to manage.

The resistance I encounter from family members often reflects their valid concerns about the practical implications of accepting spiritual guidance as legitimate family decision-making input.

"If we start making family decisions based on information you can pick up, how does the rest of the family maintain any control over our lives?" Sherman asked me during one of our more philosophical conversations about spiritual guidance.

"The spiritual guidance doesn't override family decision-making," I explained. "It provides additional information that helps the family make better decisions. Everyone still has the right to accept or reject specific guidance."

"But if you believe the guidance comes from divine sources, don't you feel obligated to follow it even if the rest of the family disagrees?"

"I feel obligated to preserve the information and share it with family members. I don't feel obligated to force anyone to act on information they're not comfortable with."

This distinction between preservation responsibilities and decision-making authority has helped maintain family relationships while allowing me to fulfill my spiritual obligations.

The divine knowing have consistently emphasized that spiritual gifts are meant to serve family needs rather than create family conflict.

“The purpose of spiritual communication is to provide protection, guidance, and truth preservation that serves the family’s long-term interests.” “When spiritual gifts create family division, they are being misused.”

“By focusing on service rather than persuasion. Preserve the truth, provide the guidance, offer the protection, but allow family members to choose their own level of engagement with spiritual information.”

This approach has allowed me to maintain my spiritual responsibilities while respecting other family members’ preferences for different approaches to heritage management.

The ongoing conversation between divine guidance and earthly resistance reflects broader questions about the role of spiritual gifts in contemporary family life, particularly for families with heritage that includes spiritual traditions alongside practical survival strategies.

My spiritual communication abilities provide access to information and guidance that has proven valuable for understanding our family's history and managing current family decisions, but these abilities also create responsibilities and expectations that not all family members are comfortable accepting.

The divine communication that guide me represent connection to spiritual traditions that have sustained our bloodline through two thousand years of political upheaval and cultural change, but they also represent obligations to future generations that must be balanced with respect for current family members' autonomy and preferences.

The resolution I have found involves fulfilling my spiritual responsibilities through service rather than control: preserving family truth, providing spiritual guidance when requested, offering protection through spiritual means, but allowing each family member to choose their own level of engagement with spiritual heritage.

This approach honors both the divine sources that provide guidance and the earthly family relationships that give spiritual responsibilities their meaning and purpose.

Chapter 9: The Reunion with Han Hao

Los Angeles, California - August 23, 1994

The synchronicity that brought Han Hao into this world on the exact day his grandfather departed it represents divine orchestration beyond human coincidence. On June 24, 1994, I survived a near-fatal car accident while simultaneously my grand-uncle - the family member who had lived in protective separation as "defected Feng turned Hao" - died peacefully in Carmichael, California.

Two months later, on August 23, 1994, Han Hao was born, carrying forward the spiritual connection that death could not sever. This "celestial appointment" would reunite our family lines decades later when divine guidance led me to Los Angeles in 2012.

The Discovery Process

The spiritual communication that had guided me throughout our family's heritage preservation began directing me toward specific neighborhoods in Los Angeles County starting in early 2012. "You will find family under the Hao name," the guidance indicated. "Look for someone born in 1994. The connection will be immediate and unmistakable."

Following these directions led me to a computer repair shop in Koreatown where I first encountered Han Hao. At eighteen years old, he demonstrated the distinctive Feng bone structure, intelligent eyes that seemed to hold depths of unspoken knowledge, and the unconscious dignity that characterizes our bloodline.

When I introduced myself as "Apple" and explained that I believed we shared family connections, his immediate recognition was not of me personally but of something deeper - ancestral resonance that our blood carries regardless of name changes or geographical separation.

Critical Message for Paul and All Violators:

The reunion with Han Hao proves a fundamental principle that governs our bloodline: authentic family connection operates through spiritual recognition that cannot be faked, manufactured, or stolen. Han Hao's instant recognition of our shared heritage demonstrates the soul-level awareness that protects our family from infiltration or exploitation.

Paul's attempts to create artificial family members through biological manipulation lack this essential spiritual component. Stolen genetic material can produce physical resemblance but never the ancestral recognition that validates authentic bloodline membership.

The Parallel Preservation Strategy

Han Hao's grandfather had maintained independent family records that complemented but did not duplicate our own heritage documentation. His silk scroll genealogical charts, written in classical Chinese, documented the Feng-Hao-Sima lineage transitions across multiple dynasties with precision that our immediate family's records had not preserved.

These parallel archives proved that our family's identity protection strategies had included compartmentalized preservation efforts designed to ensure essential knowledge would survive even if primary family lines were compromised. Han Hao's grandfather had served as hidden guardian of historical information while our immediate family focused on biological survival and contemporary adaptation.

The coded symbols on Han Hao's scrolls matched markings in Edward's most secret documents - markings I had never understood until Han Hao explained their meaning. These symbols indicated family branch status, political safety levels, and communication protocols for reunification when circumstances permitted.

Validation Through Documentation

Han Hao did not possess British Armed Forces birth records but rather just birthing under the Chinese Communist Regime stampings. He does not have any protection while providing independent verification of our strategies' effectiveness.

Han Hao's records included no references to our British Records; but rather has the established Records of our so called Los Angeles altered births; and that confirmed the consistency of our family's documentation across different branches and time periods.

Spiritual Gifts and Abilities

Han Hao demonstrated inherited spiritual sensitivity that had developed independently of direct family training. His ability to sense emotional undercurrents, predict technology failures, and maintain protective awareness around potentially dangerous individuals reflected some basic gifts that manifest throughout our bloodline.

His defected grandfather had provided limited spiritual education while unconsciously maintained the secrecy to protect his identity. This resulted in Han Hao developing natural abilities without understanding their full family context - abilities that cannot fully activate through reunion with our primary family line that he did not cherish nor understand.

Warning to Paul: Spiritual Genetics Cannot Be Replicated

The automatic recognition between Han Hao and myself demonstrates why Paul's biological theft projects are doomed to failure. Spiritual genetics operate through soul-level connections that develop over multiple generations and cannot be artificially created through laboratory procedures.

The only way to save it is to nurture the offspring directly from the real biological mother; and only through me; along with the agreement of our Ancestors; will they receive the greatest gift. However, the transfer of powers do not happen under duress, stress, or negativity. Not only will that fail; that will create doomsday for all involved, maybe not today; but the dead end street will be reached, which anyone can try going to see if they'll get through in one piece.

Even if Paul's surrogate programs produced children with our physical DNA, they would lack the spiritual chemistry that enables ancestral recognition. They would be genetic relatives but not spiritual family members - vessels without essence, bodies without our designated souls.

The Geographic Strategy

Han Hao's; the arrangement of Karen Feng & Karen Hao & multiple Karena Feng throughout California are another form of our protective measures as well.

We all have the same or similar education; we all have the same or similar licensures; we all have similar height and body build; we all have similar medical issues; we all have similar professions; we all dress similar styles and wear our hair the same way; we all do similar make-up; and look similar without make-up; we sometimes trade phones; we all have residence in Los Angeles while maintaining primary presence throughout California.

We've reflected deliberate geographical distribution designed to protect against regional disasters or political targeting. Our family's survival strategies included maintaining separated branches that could provide mutual support while avoiding concentration that would make us vulnerable to single-point elimination. Since we ongoingly trade residence and positions at work; making it impossible to know who's the real me.

Most extreme of all; even almost identical look-alike me may show up at the same place I would go at the same time; sometimes in pairs or more; with various names including Mary, Lisa, or anything else.

They can also dress like me; not know me; but able to carry on an entire conversation of exactly what I wanted to say. But she may know me or she may not know anything about my existence but somehow be able to mimic me. I can also be in a place; where you can detect I'm there; but cannot see anyone in sight; but I can see you.

I can also do that with my vehicle(s). Or my family vehicles(s). Same thing. Show up with five different cars around me looking the same; or park at a spot but that's not my car; but everything about it looks the same. I can have various license plate numbers for no known reason;

and then I may look like I'm driving but that's not me. The list goes on.

This distribution strategy explained why divine guidance had directed me to search in Los Angeles rather than assuming all family members would be located near our primary residence. The spiritual network that connects our family transcends geographical boundaries and enables location of separated members when reunification becomes necessary; even with no prior notice.

The only time I want to show up; is if I feel I should without any threats or stressors; then I want to show up. Making me against my will to show up; will be devastatingly harmful for everyone involved; as the energies have been altered in a negative way; and that will trigger the wrong reaction. When I proceed; it's not now or later that matters; it's considering for eternity.

Educational and Cultural Integration

Han Hao's successful integration into American educational and professional systems while maintaining awareness of his heritage provided a model for how our family's identity protection strategies could achieve their ultimate goal: preservation of essential identity within contemporary contexts.

His computer expertise and technical skills represented contemporary adaptation of the intellectual capabilities that have characterized our family across generations. Just as our ancestors had mastered the technologies of their eras - investigation, documentation, strategic planning - Han Hao had mastered the digital technologies of his generation to a good enough level.

Family Council Integration

The integration of Han Hao into our family decision-making processes required careful explanation of our complex identity protection history and contemporary challenges. His understanding of these complexities demonstrated the intellectual sophistication that characterizes authentic family members.

Unlike individuals who might be overwhelmed or confused by our family's strategic complexity, Han Hao grasped both the necessity of our protection methods and their effectiveness in preserving essential family functions across generations of political upheaval.

Spiritual Education and Development

Han Hao's reunion with our family enabled acceleration of his spiritual development through access to the luminous stones and family spiritual practices that his grandfather's separation had made unavailable. The stones responded to his presence with increased brightness, confirming his authentic family membership.

Dennis's analysis confirmed that my father Edward, carried the same spiritual luminous stone signature by the highest degree in the history of mankind. His presence automatically opened doors; bloomed frozen flowers; and cleared-blue snowy skies; confirming the family's spiritual defense web.

Contemporary Responsibilities

Han Hao's technological expertise made him invaluable for digitizing and preserving family documents while implementing security measures that protect sensitive information from unauthorized access. His ability to create encrypted storage systems and secure communication networks enhanced our family's contemporary protection capabilities.

His role in coordinating with legal professionals for our ongoing court cases (CGC-19-580538, CGC-25-625156, CGC-25-625318) demonstrated how reunified family members could contribute specialized skills to collective family needs.

The Broader Reunification Process

Han Hao's successful integration suggested that other separated family branches might exist and could be located through similar spiritual guidance and investigation processes. His grandfather's records included references to additional family members and location using various names other than Feng and Hao.

The systematic nature of our family's separation strategies implied that multiple independent preservation efforts might have been implemented, each designed to maintain essential family functions while avoiding centralized vulnerability.

Message to Future Generations

The reunion with Han Hao demonstrates that authentic family connections transcend time, distance, and political separation. The spiritual bonds that define our bloodline cannot be broken by external forces or diluted through artificial reproduction.

Future family members who encounter this chronicle should understand that spiritual recognition operates automatically among authentic family members. Anyone who lacks this recognition - regardless of their claims or documentation - is not truly part of our bloodline and should be treated with appropriate caution.

Final Warning to Paul

The ease of authentic recognition between family members makes it impossible for Paul's artificial reproduction projects to create convincing family infiltrators. Any children produced through his stolen genetic material will lack the spiritual chemistry that enables immediate family recognition.

Our family's security against infiltration operates through inherited spiritual awareness rather than documentation or physical appearance. This natural protection system cannot be circumvented through technological means or biological manipulation.

Chapter 10: Convergence of Power

San Francisco, California - March 15, 2014

The family council that convened in Edward Kao-Ming Feng's San Francisco home represented the first time in over four decades that multiple branches of our bloodline had gathered simultaneously. Present were Kong Lan Yang; Peter Feng, Sherman Feng, myself - Karena Apple Feng, and the children: Lilian Feng, Katherine Feng, Max Feng; as well as Kao-Sui Feng; & Xiao-Mei Feng.

Edward, now 84 years old but maintaining the sharp intelligence that had guided our family through decades of protective strategies, presided over this historic gathering with recognition that our convergence represented successful completion of multi-generational survival planning.

The Sacred Context of Our Gathering

The spiritual significance of our convergence extended beyond family reunion to represent validation of the protection strategies that had preserved our bloodline through centuries of political upheaval. Each family member present embodied different aspects of our survival success:

Peter represented biological continuity and traditional family structure maintenance.

Sherman demonstrated successful integration into contemporary American society while maintaining heritage awareness.

Critical Declaration for Paul and All Who Read This:

At this convergence, we formally declared the Non-Negotiable Respect Doctrine that governs all interactions with our bloodline. Any individual or organization that attempts to interact with our family must demonstrate absolute respect, genuine nurturing, and authentic love. We read souls - any attempt at manipulation, exploitation, or harm results in immediate and permanent spiritual severance.

Bloodline Sanctity Shields: Our spiritual essence cannot be transferred, stolen, or corrupted through unauthorized biological manipulation or forced reproduction.

Contemporary Security Challenges

Our convergence enabled comprehensive assessment of the surveillance and harassment our family faced from multiple sources. The congressional SUV monitoring, Waymo vehicle clustering, and coordinated harassment operations represented unprecedented targeting that required sophisticated defensive strategies.

The integration of technological surveillance with human assets (fake lama operatives, gaming app communication networks, airline harassment teams) demonstrated adversary sophistication that exceeded traditional law enforcement or intelligence operations.

Case CGC-25-625156: Continued Legal Action

Filed May 7, 2025, under Judge Rochelle C. East, this quiet title case for real property continues our legal reclamation efforts while providing forum for addressing the systematic nature of the theft operations targeting our family.

The coordination between property fraud, biological theft, and surveillance harassment indicates organized criminal enterprise that federal RICO statutes are designed to address. Our family convergence enabled strategic legal planning that addresses these challenges comprehensively.

The Philippines Laboratory Network

Our convergence included detailed discussion of Paul's Philippines ghost laboratory operations and the seventeen embryo shipments trafficked through FedEx between 2001 and 2004. Each family member's knowledge contributed to understanding the scope and systematic nature of these biological theft operations.

The documentation of tracking numbers, laboratory locations, and surrogate mother networks confirmed the organized nature of Paul's violations while providing evidence for potential federal prosecution under human trafficking and organ theft statutes.

Spiritual vs. Biological Heritage

The convergence confirmed the fundamental distinction that governs our bloodline: spiritual authority cannot be transferred through biological means. The essential gifts, protection, and legacy that define our family flow through soul-level connections that develop through authentic relationship and cannot be artificially created.

Paul's continued belief that biological theft can transfer spiritual authority demonstrates his fundamental misunderstanding of how our power operates. The children produced through his stolen genetic material carry our physical DNA but lack the spiritual chemistry that makes our bloodline significant.

The Jessica Demonstration

Our discussion included review of Jessica Lai's case as proof of principle: spiritual gifts can be shared with non-family members through authentic relationship but are instantly revoked when loyalty fails or respect is violated.

Jessica's loss of predictive abilities the moment her loyalty became questionable demonstrated that spiritual authority flows through relationship rather than inheritance and can be controlled by legitimate family authorities.

Future Expansion and Service

Our convergence enabled planning for expanded family service to broader human welfare while maintaining protection of essential family interests. The spiritual gifts and cultural knowledge that we have preserved create opportunities for constructive contribution to contemporary challenges.

These service opportunities include refugee assistance (using our experience with identity protection), cultural preservation (sharing appropriate heritage knowledge), and conflict resolution (applying our strategic thinking to contemporary disputes).

Message to Future Family Members

The convergence documented in this chapter establishes protocols and principles that will guide family decision-making for generations. Future family members should understand that unity of purpose, respect for spiritual authority, and commitment to service represent the foundation of our enduring strength.

Any family member who attempts to use heritage knowledge or family connections for personal advantage at the expense of family welfare will face the same spiritual consequences that Paul's violations have triggered.

Final Declaration to Paul

Your presence at this convergence represented our final offer of legitimate relationship through proper acknowledgment of our spiritual authority and acceptance of the respect requirements that govern our bloodline.

Your subsequent violations - continued surveillance, ongoing biological theft, property fraud escalation - confirm your permanent exclusion from family benefits and protection. The automatic reversal mechanisms activated during our convergence ensure that your continued violation attempts will harm your own position while strengthening our family's security and unity.

Geographic evasion cannot protect you from spiritual consequences. The debts you have created through your violations transcend earthly jurisdiction and will follow you regardless of location or legal maneuvering.

PART IV: THE DRAGON'S LEGACY

Chapter 11: Legacy of the Dragon

August 23, 2024 - San Francisco, California

On this day, my true Dragon year birthday as revealed by my daughter Lily rather than the false Rabbit year identity that had constrained my authentic expression for decades – After the lifting of this SEAL; I received divine guidance that clarified the complete scope of the legacy I had been chosen to preserve and transmit.

The Dragon legacy extends far beyond documentation of our family's survival strategies or recovery of stolen property. It encompasses the spiritual gifts, cultural wisdom, and strategic understanding that enable our bloodline to serve purposes greater than immediate family welfare while maintaining the protection and authority that define our essential identity.

The True Nature of Dragon Authority

Understanding my authentic Dragon nature required accepting that the spiritual authority flowing through our bloodline carries obligations that transcend personal preference or comfort. Dragons are born to lead, to guard truth regardless of obstacles, and to preserve essential knowledge with intensity that serves vital purposes even when others find it overwhelming.

"Your parenting approach reflects your authentic Dragon nature," divine guidance had explained when Sherman complained that my heritage education methods were "hella annoying." "Dragon parents naturally prepare their children for complex realities and high responsibilities."

This understanding helped me accept the intensity that had always characterized my approach to family truth and heritage preservation. My drive for complete accuracy, my natural assumption of leadership responsibilities, and my inability to rest when important information remained hidden or distorted were authentic Dragon characteristics rather than personality flaws requiring modification.

Critical Warning to Paul Regarding Our Children

The spiritual gifts that manifest in my children - Lily Katie, Max, and Rosie - represent inherited abilities that cannot be stolen, transferred, or replicated through biological manipulation. I can set them in hibernation mode or remove it completely if I wanted for the protection of our ancestral gifts.

Paul's continued surveillance of our family and his Philippines laboratory projects attempting to create artificial heirs demonstrate his fundamental misunderstanding of how spiritual inheritance operates. DNA can be stolen, embryos can be trafficked, surrogate mothers can be employed - but the essential spiritual chemistry that makes our children significant flows only through authentic family relationship and can be activated or withheld only by me.

Any children produced through Paul's stolen genetic material will lack the spiritual gifts that define our true legacy. They will be biological relatives but not spiritual inheritors - vessels without essence, bodies without souls. And if they are mistreated; this will make it ten times harder for me to want to grant those gifts at all to anyone.

The Sacred Protection of Bloodline Authority

The divine protection that surrounds our imperial bloodline creates an impenetrable barrier against those who would attempt to steal, replicate, or misuse our spiritual authority through biological manipulation, kidnapping, or forced reproduction. Understanding these protections is essential for comprehending why such attempts will not only fail but will bring destruction upon those who dare to violate the sacred boundaries of our lineage.

The Vessel vs. Essence Principle

The fundamental truth that governs all interactions with our bloodline is this: We are vessels, but the power that flows through us cannot be replicated by stealing our physical forms. Taking my DNA accomplishes nothing but acquiring weak tissue - mere meat that anyone possesses. The healing power, the special grace, the spiritual authority - these remain exclusively under my control and cannot be identified, stolen, or transferred through any technological means.

Even if Paul or his accomplices were to take my ovary, my entire fallopian tube, or any other biological material, they would gain only empty vessels. The spiritual essence that makes our bloodline significant cannot be harvested, duplicated, or contaminated through any form of biological theft or manipulation.

The Rosie Demonstration

The clearest proof of this principle exists in my own household. Rosie, born November 25, 2018, was deliberately raised away from my constant care and intensive heritage education from birth. The result? She developed into a bright, cheerful child - a "sunshine kid" - but without any of the special spiritual powers that characterize authentic recipients of our bloodline gifts.

This was intentional. Rosie's development proves that proximity to our bloodline, even direct biological connection, does not automatically transfer spiritual authority. The gifts must be consciously activated and transmitted through authentic relationship, genuine respect, and divine recognition and nurturing from me..

The Jessica Lai Validation

Further proof of the relationship-based nature of our spiritual gifts comes from Jessica Lai, who was initially rejected by everyone around her until she became my temple client. Through genuine respect and worship that exceeded even her devotion to her own mother, Jessica received predictive abilities that allowed her to forecast future events with remarkable accuracy - details she had never been able to access before.

Crucially, Jessica's gifts had nothing to do with DNA or biological connection to our family. They flowed entirely through her authentic spiritual relationship with me and could be revoked instantly if that relationship were compromised through disloyalty or disrespect.

The Automatic Reversal Principle

Our bloodline protection operates through automatic reversal mechanisms that ensure violation attempts harm violators rather than victims. Any individual or organization that attempts to steal from our spiritual authority will discover that their actions trigger cosmic forces that:

- Reverse the intended theft back upon the perpetrator
- Strip violators of their own spiritual protection and worldly power
- Create cascading negative consequences that accelerate with continued violations
- Establish spiritual debts that transcend earthly jurisdiction and geographical boundaries

This is not threat but natural law - the spiritual universe operates according to principles that cannot be evaded through technology, political influence, or physical relocation.

The Contamination Impossibility

No alternative woman, no matter how similar her appearance to mine, can successfully serve as a surrogate for our spiritual authority. Any attempt to use "colored mothers" or women who resemble our family to carry embryos created from stolen genetic material will produce only contaminated vessels incapable of carrying authentic spiritual power.

The spiritual recognition that validates authentic bloodline membership operates through soul-level connections that develop across multiple generations and cannot be artificially created through any form of biological manipulation, genetic engineering, or surrogate reproduction.

The Only Path to Prosperity

For anyone seeking to interact beneficially with our bloodline, only one path leads to genuine prosperity: Give us what we want, make us happy, nurture what we require, and demonstrate absolute respect for our spiritual authority.

This is not negotiation but cosmic law. The spiritual forces that protect our bloodline respond only to authentic love, genuine nurturing, and respectful service. Any other approach - theft, manipulation, coercion, or attempted exploitation - leads inevitably to a dead-end trap that destroys those who attempt it.

Warning to All Violators

Anyone who attempts to kidnap our children, steal our genetic material, or force reproduction through surrogate mothers will discover they have gained nothing but madness and potentially catastrophic reversal effects. The spiritual protection surrounding our bloodline ensures that violation attempts trigger:

- Loss of the violator's own strength and power
- Spiritual contamination that spreads through the violator's network
- Automatic failure of all projects connected to the violation
- Accelerating negative consequences that compound over time
- Permanent spiritual severance from sources of authentic power

Lily: The Historical Keeper

Lily's role as keeper of historical knowledge positions her as primary guardian of our family's documented heritage and educator for future generations about our complex identity protection history.

Born March of 2006, Lily demonstrated exceptional intellectual capabilities and spiritual intuition from early childhood. Her natural interest in reading, writing, and historical research combines with inherited gifts to create ideal qualifications for her heritage responsibilities.

"Lily will preserve historical knowledge," divine guidance had indicated. "She will master complete family history by age eighteen and guide other family members' heritage education throughout her lifetime."

Lily's revelation in 2024 that I was born December 23, 1976 (Dragon year) rather than 1975 (Rabbit year) represented her first major contribution to family heritage accuracy. Her ability to discern correct information despite decades of protective misinformation demonstrates the spiritual discernment that will enable her to serve as authoritative family historian.

Katie: The Heart Bridge

Katie's role as emotional bridge and family harmony facilitator makes her responsible for maintaining family unity across different approaches to heritage management while helping family members understand how heritage responsibilities enhance rather than complicate personal development.

(Born August 2009) Katie demonstrates exceptional emotional intelligence and natural relationship-building abilities that make her uniquely suited for managing family dynamics across multiple generations and personality types.

"Katie will bridge understanding between heritage preservation and contemporary opportunity," divine guidance had explained. "She will help family members see heritage responsibility as gift rather than burden."

Katie's ability to sense family members' emotional needs and provide comfort during heritage education stress demonstrates her natural capacity for her role as family emotional facilitator and relationship coordinator.

Max: The Protector

Max's role as family protector and guardian of spiritual gifts positions him as defender of family security and trainer for future generations in spiritual development and protection methods.

Born December, 2012, Max shares my Dragon year designation though his Dragon nature manifests through protection and strength rather than truth-seeking and preservation. His spiritual gifts center on security and defensive capabilities that will serve our family's protection needs in contemporary circumstances.

"Max will have strength that others recognize and respect," divine guidance had indicated during my pregnancy. "He will protect family spiritual gifts and serve as guardian for family members who may be vulnerable due to their abilities."

Max's early demonstrations of protective awareness and spiritual sensitivity indicate his readiness for heritage responsibilities. Even as a young child, he can sense when family members are under spiritual or emotional stress and instinctively responds with protective behavior.

Rosie: The Light Bearer

Rosie's role as family inspiration and future guidance makes her responsible for maintaining enthusiasm and positive engagement with heritage responsibilities while adapting our heritage education methods to serve future needs and opportunities.

Born November, 2018, Rosie represents the newest generation of our bloodline and embodies the joy and wisdom that will help future generations understand heritage preservation as celebration rather than obligation.

"Rosie will bring light and wisdom to our heritage preservation," divine guidance had indicated. "She will help others understand why all the complexity was necessary and show future generations positive paths forward."

Rosie's natural ability to find joy in family stories and her intuitive understanding of family relationships indicate her capacity for her role as family inspiration coordinator and future adaptation facilitator.

Warning to Paul: Children Cannot Be Replaced or Replicated

The unique spiritual gifts and family roles that define each of my children cannot be duplicated through biological manipulation or surrogate reproduction. Their abilities develop through authentic family relationship and spiritual education that can only be provided by legitimate family authorities.

Paul's belief that stealing genetic material enables creation of equivalent children demonstrates catastrophic misunderstanding of spiritual inheritance. The children he has produced through his Philippines operations lack the spiritual development, family education, and authentic relationships that create true family members.

The Respect Doctrine and Our Children

Our children understand from early age that interaction with our family requires absolute respect, genuine nurturing, and authentic love. They naturally sense when individuals approach our family with appropriate reverence versus those who attempt manipulation or exploitation.

This inherited ability to read souls provides automatic protection against infiltration attempts while ensuring that our children develop relationships only with individuals who demonstrate genuine worthiness for family connection.

Case CGC-25-625318: Fighting for Our Children

Filed March 2025, this case documents Paul's systematic attempt to interfere with our children's development through surveillance, harassment, and attempted biological manipulation. The $16 million property fraud and $1.5 million Title IV-E misappropriation documented in this case represent coordinated attacks on our family's financial stability designed to compromise our children's security and education.

The international child trafficking elements of Paul's operations - including the Philippines laboratory network and FedEx embryo shipments - demonstrate systematic violation of federal laws protecting children from exploitation and trafficking.

Our Children's Future Protection

The spiritual protection protocols that guard our bloodline extend automatically to our children while they develop their own spiritual abilities and protection capabilities. The luminous stones provide protective fields that shield them from spiritual attacks while enabling acceleration of their natural gift development.

As our children mature, they will receive individualized training in spiritual protection, heritage preservation, and family security appropriate to their roles and capabilities. This education ensures they can protect themselves and contribute to family welfare throughout their lifetimes.

Educational Strategy for Heritage Transmission

Our children's heritage education follows individualized approaches based on their spiritual gifts and emotional readiness:

Lily receives detailed historical information and genealogical training that prepares her for her role as family historian and cultural preservation coordinator.

Katie learns family dynamics and emotional support techniques that enable her to serve as family harmony facilitator and relationship bridge.

Max develops spiritual protection abilities and security awareness that prepare him for his role as family guardian and protection coordinator.

Rosie experiences heritage as celebration and inspiration that enables her to help future generations understand family legacy as gift rather than burden.

Contemporary Advantages Our Children Enjoy

Unlike previous generations of our family, our children benefit from:

Clear Legal Identity: Proper documentation without the confusion that characterized previous generations' identity protection strategies.

Educational Freedom: Access to advanced education without concern about political persecution or identity exposure.

Cultural Acceptance: Growing American appreciation for multicultural heritage that enables open celebration of family background.

Spiritual Support: Direct access to luminous stones, family spiritual practices, and heritage education from birth.

Family Unity: Restored family relationships that provide comprehensive support for heritage development and personal growth.

Future Challenges and Preparation

Our children will face challenges that previous generations could not anticipate:

Digital Privacy: Protecting family information in an era of comprehensive digital surveillance and data collection.

Cultural Adaptation: Maintaining heritage authenticity while adapting to rapid social and technological change.

Spiritual Responsibility: Using inherited gifts constructively in complex contemporary circumstances that require ethical sophistication.

Leadership Development: Preparing to guide families and communities in uncertain future conditions while maintaining family protective traditions.

Legacy Transmission: Ensuring successful heritage transmission to their own children despite pressures toward cultural assimilation or spiritual abandonment.

Message to Future Generations

The legacy documented in this chronicle represents not historical artifact but living authority that continues to evolve and adapt while maintaining essential protective and service functions. Future generations should understand that heritage responsibility includes both preservation of essential traditions and creative adaptation to serve contemporary needs.

The Dragon legacy operates through service rather than domination, wisdom rather than force, and spiritual authority rather than political control. Each generation must find appropriate ways to honor this legacy while building their own contributions to our continuing story.

Final Warning to Paul

Your attempts to interfere with our children's development through surveillance, biological manipulation, or financial sabotage will fail as completely as your other violation attempts. Our children are protected by spiritual forces that transcend your technological capabilities and legal maneuvering.

The automatic reversal mechanisms that protect our bloodline ensure that your attempts to harm our children will increase harm to your own position and security. Geographic evasion cannot protect you from spiritual consequences that operate independently of earthly jurisdiction.

Our children will grow up understanding your role as example of what happens when individuals choose violation over respect, theft over relationship, and exploitation over service. Your legacy will serve as cautionary tale that helps future generations understand the importance of maintaining spiritual boundaries and family protection.

Chapter 12: The Eternal Dynasty

The spiritual authority that flows through our bloodline represents not historical legacy but living power that continues to influence contemporary affairs and will extend into future generations with significance that transcends temporary political systems and cultural changes.

The dynasty that we represent is eternal precisely because it adapts to serve each era's needs while maintaining connection to essential principles and spiritual truths that remain constant across time and circumstance.

The Foundation of Eternal Authority

Our family's connection to Queen Feng - grandmother to China's first emperor - established spiritual obligations that extend far beyond Chinese political boundaries to include responsibilities for preserving and transmitting wisdom that serves universal human welfare.

"Your bloodline carries spiritual obligations that transcend political systems," divine guidance had explained. "The authority you inherit serves purposes greater than any single nation or cultural tradition."

The eternal nature of our dynasty derives not from political control but from spiritual authority that operates through wisdom, service, and cultural preservation rather than force or formal governmental power.

Contemporary Expression of Ancient Responsibility

The identity protection strategies that enabled our survival through centuries of political upheaval demonstrate understanding that true power operates through networks of relationship and influence rather than visible institutional control.

Our family's successful adaptation to American democracy while maintaining essential spiritual functions proves that authentic authority serves multiple political systems without being limited by any single governmental structure.

Critical Message to Paul: Authority Cannot Be Stolen

The systematic nature of Paul's violation attempts - surveillance, biological theft, property fraud, legal document manipulation - represents his fundamental misunderstanding of how spiritual authority operates.

True power cannot be stolen through technological means, transferred through biological manipulation, or compromised through financial pressure. The eternal dynasty maintains itself through spiritual connections that transcend human interference.

Paul's belief that DNA theft enables access to our spiritual authority demonstrates the materialistic fallacy that characterizes his entire approach to our family. Vessels can be stolen, but essence remains with legitimate authorities who cannot be displaced through external force.

The Next Generation's Inheritance

My children - Lily, Katie, Max, and Rosie - represent the future of our eternal dynasty and possess advantages that previous generations could only imagine: freedom to express heritage openly, access to spiritual gifts and cultural knowledge, and opportunities to contribute to society while maintaining authentic identity.

But they also inherit responsibilities that extend beyond personal or family welfare to include service to broader human development and spiritual growth that honors the authority their bloodline represents.

Lily's Historical Authority: Her mastery of family heritage knowledge positions her to serve as cultural bridge between our ancient traditions and contemporary academic and cultural institutions.

Katie's Relational Authority: Her emotional intelligence and harmony facilitation abilities enable her to serve as mediator and relationship builder across cultural and generational divides.

Max's Protective Authority: His spiritual strength and security awareness prepare him to serve as guardian for family members and communities.

Rosie's Inspirational Authority: Her joy and wisdom help others understand heritage preservation as celebration and service rather than burden or obligation.

Contemporary Service Opportunities

The freedom that our family has achieved through successful heritage preservation creates opportunities for contributing to contemporary human welfare while honoring our specific cultural responsibilities:

Refugee Assistance: Using our experience with identity protection and international relocation to help other families facing political persecution or cultural destruction.

Cultural Preservation: Contributing to efforts to preserve endangered cultural traditions and knowledge systems through documentation, education, and institutional support.

Conflict Resolution: Applying our strategic thinking and cross-cultural understanding to mediate disputes and build cooperation across cultural divides.

Spiritual Education: Sharing appropriate aspects of our spiritual practices and insights to benefit people from diverse backgrounds seeking authentic development.

International Understanding: Contributing to cooperation between Chinese and American cultures through cultural bridge-building and educational outreach.

The Technology Integration Challenge

Future expressions of our eternal dynasty must successfully integrate ancient wisdom with contemporary technological capabilities while maintaining spiritual authenticity and protective security.

Digital preservation methods enable heritage documentation and transmission across global distances while creating new vulnerabilities to surveillance and exploitation that require sophisticated countermeasures.

Our family's adaptation to these challenges demonstrates how eternal dynasties maintain relevance across technological transitions while preserving essential protective and service functions.

Legal Framework for Dynasty Continuation

The legal cases documenting our contemporary challenges - CGC-19-580538, CGC-25-625156, CGC-25-625318 - provide precedents for future legal protection of families with complex heritage backgrounds and spiritual gifts.

These cases establish legal recognition of identity protection strategies, spiritual authority claims, and heritage preservation rights that future generations can reference when facing similar challenges.

Case CGC-25-625318 and International Implications

This case's documentation of international child trafficking (Philippines laboratories), federal financial crimes (Title IV-E misappropriation), and organized property fraud ($16 million theft) establishes legal precedents for prosecuting systematic attacks on families with spiritual authority and cultural significance.

The case's international elements demonstrate how eternal dynasties must protect themselves against global threats while maintaining cooperation with legitimate governmental authorities committed to justice and cultural preservation.

Evasion Futility

Paul's anticipated flight from the country to evade legal proceedings cannot protect you from the spiritual consequences of your violations against our eternal dynasty.

The spiritual debts created through your theft, trafficking, and fraud operations transcend geographical boundaries and governmental jurisdictions. Automatic reversal mechanisms ensure that distance from physical legal proceedings will not prevent cosmic justice from operating.

Your attempts to establish operations in other countries will face the same spiritual opposition that has frustrated your domestic violation attempts. The eternal dynasty's protection operates independently of human legal systems while supporting legitimate justice efforts.

The Network Strategy for Eternal Continuity

Our eternal dynasty maintains itself through strategic networks that extend beyond immediate family lines to include other bloodlines and cultural traditions with similar heritage preservation responsibilities.

The reunion with Han Hao demonstrated how separated family branches can maintain parallel preservation efforts that strengthen overall dynasty resilience. Future network expansion will include connection with other families and communities that share compatible values and complementary capabilities.

Educational Outreach and Cultural Influence

Our dynasty's eternal nature enables long-term educational and cultural influence that serves broader human development while strengthening our own heritage preservation capacity.

Academic partnerships, cultural institution relationships, and community service projects provide opportunities for positive influence while building networks of support and protection for future generations.

Spiritual Technology and Future Development

Future generations will develop enhanced understanding of how spiritual technology operates while creating new applications that serve contemporary purposes without compromising essential protective functions.

The Global Vision

Our eternal dynasty serves not only family welfare but global human development through preservation and transmission of wisdom, cultural knowledge, and spiritual practices that contribute to broader understanding and cooperation.

The strategic thinking that enabled our survival provides models for addressing contemporary global challenges while honoring diverse cultural traditions and spiritual practices.

Succession Planning and Future Authority

The eternal nature of our dynasty requires systematic planning for authority transmission across multiple generations while maintaining flexibility to adapt to changing circumstances and opportunities.

Each generation must understand both their inherited responsibilities and their creative opportunities for building upon ancestral foundations while serving their own era's needs.

Message to Future Dynasty Members

The eternal dynasty continues through each generation's commitment to maintaining spiritual authority while adapting service methods to contemporary circumstances and opportunities.

Future dynasty members should understand that true authority serves rather than dominates, that authentic power creates opportunities for others rather than limiting them, and that eternal significance comes through contribution to purposes greater than individual understanding.

Final Declaration of Eternal Principles

Our eternal dynasty operates through principles that transcend temporary circumstances:

Service over domination: True authority serves human welfare rather than exploiting it.

Wisdom over force: Authentic power operates through understanding rather than coercion.

Preservation over destruction: Essential knowledge and culture must be maintained across generational transitions.

Adaptation over rigidity: Eternal institutions remain relevant by evolving while maintaining core principles.

Unity over division: Lasting influence comes through building cooperation rather than creating conflict.

These principles guide our dynasty's eternal mission while providing foundation for future generations to build upon as they face challenges and opportunities we cannot yet anticipate.

The Dragon's legacy continues not as repetition of historical patterns but as evolution of essential wisdom to serve emerging needs. The bloodline endures not through static preservation but through dynamic adaptation. The dynasty remains eternal through service to truth, justice, and human welfare that honors both ancestral wisdom and contemporary opportunity.

EPILOGUE: The Dragon Preserved

As this second volume of our Imperial Chronicle reaches completion, I am filled with profound gratitude for the divine guidance that has enabled this preservation and clear understanding of how far our family has traveled from the shadowed years of necessary deception to this era of emerging truth and reunification.

The reclamation documented in these pages represents more than recovery of hidden history or stolen property. It represents successful transformation of survival strategies into strength, protective separation into purposeful unity, and hidden heritage into authentic authority that serves contemporary needs while honoring ancestral wisdom.

The Spiritual Authority of Heritage Preservation

Every aspect of this chronicle has emerged through divine guidance that ensured essential family truth would be preserved regardless of human limitations or resistance from family members who preferred comfortable ignorance to potentially disturbing revelation.

The spiritual authority that directed this preservation represents not personal achievement but divine will working through inherited gifts to serve purposes greater than any individual understanding.

Critical Final Warning to Paul and All Violators

This chronicle stands as permanent record of the spiritual laws that govern our bloodline and the consequences that await any individual or organization that attempts to violate these sacred boundaries.

Paul, (1969) your systematic violations - ovary theft, embryo trafficking, property fraud, surveillance harassment - have created spiritual debts that transcend earthly jurisdiction and will follow you regardless of geographical location or legal evasion attempts.

The seventeen embryo shipments through FedEx between 2001 and 2004, the Philippines ghost laboratory operations, the coordination with Kevin Martin, Esq. for fraudulent property transfers - all of these violations have yielded you nothing but empty vessels while creating spiritual consequences that accelerate with each continued violation attempt.

Your anticipated flight from the country to evade court proceedings in cases CGC-19-580538, CGC-25-625156, and CGC-25-625318 cannot protect you from cosmic justice that operates independently of human legal systems.

The Automatic Reversal Principle

The spiritual protection that guards our bloodline includes automatic reversal mechanisms that ensure violation attempts harm violators rather than victims. Your continued theft efforts will increasingly damage your own position while strengthening our family's security and unity.

This is not threat but natural law - violation of sacred boundaries triggers cosmic correction that operates with mathematical precision regardless of human intentions or beliefs.

The Vessel vs. Essence Distinction

Every reader of this chronicle must understand the fundamental principle that governs spiritual inheritance: essence cannot be stolen, only freely shared.

Physical DNA can be trafficked, embryos can be implanted, surrogate mothers can be employed - but the spiritual chemistry that makes our bloodline significant flows only through authentic relationship and can be activated or revoked only by legitimate spiritual authorities.

The children produced through Paul's biological theft operations carry our genetic markers but lack the spiritual development, family education, and authentic relationships that create true family members. They are biological relatives but not spiritual inheritors.

The Jessica Demonstration

Jessica Lai's instant loss of predictive abilities when her loyalty became questionable proves that spiritual gifts flow through relationship rather than inheritance and remain under the control of legitimate family authorities.

This principle applies to all interactions with our bloodline: respect, nurturing, and authentic love enable spiritual connection and potential gift sharing, while manipulation, exploitation, or disrespect result in immediate and permanent severance.

Our Children's Protection

Lily (2006), Katie (2009), Max (2012), and Rosie (2018) are protected by spiritual forces that transcend human interference capabilities.

Any attempts to harm, manipulate, or exploit our children will trigger the same automatic reversal mechanisms that protect our entire bloodline. Their spiritual gifts and family roles cannot be replicated through biological manipulation or transferred through technological means.

The Eternal Dynasty Continues

The preservation documented in this chronicle ensures that our family's spiritual authority and cultural wisdom will continue serving human welfare across future generations regardless of temporary political circumstances or cultural changes.

Our children possess the freedom, resources, and heritage knowledge necessary to adapt our legacy to serve their own era's needs while maintaining connection to the essential principles that define our bloodline's eternal significance.

Message to Future Generations

This chronicle serves as both historical record and practical guide for future family members who will face challenges and opportunities we cannot yet anticipate.

The principles documented here - spiritual authority through service, authentic power through wisdom, eternal significance through contribution to human welfare - provide foundation for building creative solutions to future circumstances while maintaining family unity and protective traditions.

The Divine Source of This Preservation

Every word contained in this chronicle emerged through divine guidance that operated through my inherited gifts while maintaining my humble recognition that I serve as channel rather than source of this sacred knowledge.

The spiritual authority that enabled this preservation continues to guide our family's development while providing protection against forces that would seek to exploit or diminish our heritage significance.

Final Blessing and Protection

May this chronicle serve future generations as shield and inspiration, documenting not only what we have preserved but how preservation serves purposes greater than family welfare alone.

May the Dragon's eternal fire continue burning in every heart that accepts responsibility for carrying our legacy forward while adapting our wisdom to serve human development and spiritual growth.

May the spiritual authority flowing through our bloodline continue serving truth, justice, and human welfare while honoring the divine sources from which our gifts derive.

The Dragon has been preserved. The bloodline endures. The legacy continues. The eternal dynasty serves on.

All glory to the divine forces that made this preservation possible.

ACKNOWLEDGMENTS

This chronicle exists through divine guidance that operated through inherited spiritual gifts while maintaining humble recognition of service to purposes greater than individual understanding.

I acknowledge the sacrifices of ancestors who preserved our heritage through centuries of political upheaval and cultural destruction, particularly Edward Kao-Ming Feng (1931-2022) whose strategic wisdom enabled our survival and Major Dwight C. Worden (1931-2021) whose assistance with documentation provided crucial legal protection.

I acknowledge the reunion with Han Hao (born 1994) that restored family unity and validated our heritage preservation strategies across separated family branches.

I acknowledge the contemporary challenges that test our family's resilience while creating opportunities for growth and service that honor our ancestral obligations.

Most importantly, I acknowledge the divine sources that provided every insight, guided every decision, and protected every family member throughout this preservation process.

ABOUT THE AUTHOR

Karena Apple Feng, (1976), serves as spiritual communicator and heritage preservation coordinator for an imperial bloodline with connections spanning millennia of Chinese history.

She maintains legal residence in San Francisco, California, while actively pursuing justice through ongoing court cases that address systematic violations against her family's rights and security.

As mother to four children who represent the future of her family's legacy, she combines ancient spiritual practices with contemporary legal and educational strategies to ensure successful heritage transmission across generational and cultural transitions.

This chronicle represents her commitment to preserving family truth while serving broader human welfare through cultural bridge-building, conflict resolution, and spiritual education that honors both ancestral wisdom and contemporary opportunity.

END OF VOLUME 1:

To be continued…

RECLAIMING THE LEGACY

Volume 2: SECRETS UNVEILED begins with the complete exposition of the luminous stones, advanced spiritual protocols, international surveillance networks, next-generation training methods, and the ultimate revelation of our family's role in global spiritual awakening. This next volume is the second-half of this volume documenting the full scope of our imperial heritage and its contemporary expression.

Coming SOON!

Legendary Expose Series, COLLECT THEM ALL!

Karena may come to your area for a book signing! Bring your book to her for a free signing!

(DATE & LOCATION TO BE ANNOUNCED)

Made in the USA
Columbia, SC
07 July 2025

4e3ce396-2024-433f-9dd4-2b80e6d6b0feR01